Discovering Spheres

Nancy Furstinger and John Willis

www.av2books.com

3 2401 00910 788 1

AV² provides enriched content that supplements and complements this book. Weigl's AV² books strive to create inspired learning and engage young minds in a total learning experience.

Your AV² Media Enhanced books come alive with...

 **Audio** Listen to sections of the book read aloud.

 **Key Words** Study vocabulary, and complete a matching word activity.

Go to www.av2books.com, and enter this book's unique code.

BOOK CODE

V745234

 **Video** Watch informative video clips.

 **Quizzes** Test your knowledge.

 **Embedded Weblinks** Gain additional information for research.

 **Slide Show** View images and captions, and prepare a presentation.

AV² by Weigl brings you media enhanced books that support active learning.

 **Try This!** Complete activities and hands-on experiments.

... and much, much more

Published by AV² by Weigl
350 5th Avenue, 59th Floor
New York, NY 10118
www.av2books.com

Copyright © 2017 AV² by Weigl
All rights reserved. No part of this publication may be reproduced, stored in a retrieval system, or transmitted in any form or by any means, electronic, mechanical, photocopying, recording, or otherwise, without the prior written permission of the publisher.

Library of Congress Cataloging-in-Publication Data

Names: Furstinger, Nancy. | Willis, John, 1989- , author.
Title: Discovering spheres / Nancy Furstinger and John Willis.
Description: New York, NY : AV2 by Weigl, [2017] | Series: 3D objects | Includes index.
Identifiers: LCCN 2016005643 (print) | LCCN 2016015448 (ebook) | ISBN 9781489649867 (hard cover : alk. paper) | ISBN 9781489649874 (soft cover : alk. paper) | ISBN 9781489649881 (Multi-user ebk.)
Subjects: LCSH: Sphere--Juvenile literature. | Shapes--Juvenile literature. | Geometry, Solid--Juvenile literature.
Classification: LCC QA491 .F8727 2017 (print) | LCC QA491 (ebook) | DDC 516/.154--dc23
LC record available at https://lccn.loc.gov/2016005643

Printed in the United States of America in Brainerd, Minnesota
1 2 3 4 5 6 7 8 9 0 20 19 18 17 16

082016
210716

Project Coordinator: John Willis   Art Director: Terry Paulhus

Every reasonable effort has been made to trace ownership and to obtain permission to reprint copyright material. The publishers would be pleased to have any errors or omissions brought to their attention so that they may be corrected in subsequent printings.

Weigl acknowledges Getty Images, Alamy, and iStock as its primary image suppliers for this title.

2 3D Objects

CONTENTS

AV² Book Code 2
Juggling Balls and Juice 4
What Does a Sphere Look Like? 6
How Do We Know If a Shape is a Sphere? 8
Parts of a Sphere 9
Spheres at Play 10
Old-Time Games.. 11
Spheres We Eat.. 12
Sweet Spheres 14
Largest Bubble Gum Bubble Blown............. 15
Building Spheres.. 16
Spheres in Space 17
Spheres for All Seasons.................................. 18
Spheres Quiz.. 20
Activity: Bubble Fun 22
Key Words/Index... 23
Log on to www.av2books.com 24

JUGGLING BALLS AND JUICE

At a street festival, you spy a juggler. She juggles five balls higher and higher in the air. You get dizzy just watching her.

Next, you play a carnival game. You have three softballs to throw. You hit the target. You choose a large, fuzzy ball for your prize.

Did you know that oranges start out with a green-colored peel? They turn orange when the weather gets cool.

3D Objects

At a nearby booth, you order fresh-squeezed orange juice. You watch the bright, juicy oranges tumble into the squeezing machine. Did you notice how the shape of the balls matches the shape of the oranges? Both of these shapes are **spheres**.

Spheres are easy to hold if they are the right size. This makes them great shapes for juggling.

Spheres 5

WHAT DOES A SPHERE LOOK LIKE?

Sphere shapes are all around us. Spheres have three **dimensions**. They are not flat like circles. Circles and flat shapes have only two dimensions, length and width. Flat shapes are also called **plane** shapes or 2D shapes.

Spheres and other shapes that have three dimensions are **3D** shapes. 3D shapes are also called solid shapes.

Tennis balls are made of hollow rubber spheres, covered in felt.

3D Objects

Spheres 7

HOW DO WE KNOW IF A SHAPE IS A SPHERE?

Spheres have no top, bottom, or sides. No matter which way you turn them, their shape looks the same.

Look closely. A sphere is perfectly round, like a ball. This shape has no **edges** or corners.

A sphere has only one **surface**. It goes all around the sphere.

All points on the surface of the sphere are the same distance from the center.

3D Objects

PARTS OF A SPHERE

A sphere has no edges or corners.

Spheres

SPHERES AT PLAY

Now you can easily spot this 3D shape. You will see spheres everywhere you go.

You meet your friends at the playground. Some are playing a game of soccer. Others are practicing hitting softballs. One is dribbling a basketball. Two are tossing a beach ball in the pool.

All of these balls are shaped like spheres. Can you think of a ball that is not shaped like a sphere?

Your brother is playing jacks. He bounces a rubber ball, picks up jacks, and catches the ball before it bounces again. When he is bored, he can switch to a game of marbles. Your sister is blowing soap bubbles. Each bubble has colors that swirl and shimmer. What other games use sphere shapes?

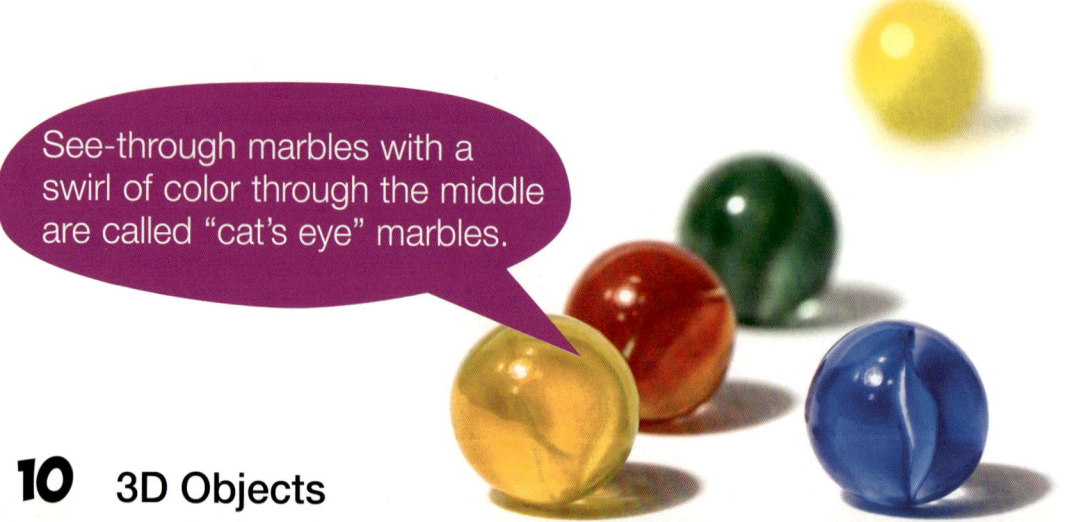

See-through marbles with a swirl of color through the middle are called "cat's eye" marbles.

OLD-TIME GAMES

Jacks was once called knucklebones because it was played with sheep bones more than 2,000 years ago. Today, this game of skill is played with pointy metal jacks and a bouncing ball.

The game of marbles has been popular for 3,000 years. Shooter and playing marbles were made of clay, stone, or marble. Today, kids play with a rainbow of glass marbles.

Spheres are everywhere. Can you spot the little spheres on the pointy jacks?

Spheres

SPHERES WE EAT

Some spheres are juicy. When you visit the supermarket, explore the **produce** section. Many fruits have this 3D shape. You can squeeze oranges, tangerines, and grapefruits into juices. Watch a grown-up slice cantaloupe and honeydew melons. Pop blueberries in your mouth.

Many fruits and vegetables are shaped like spheres, including blueberries. Can you think of any other foods that are sphere-shaped?

12   3D Objects

Many vegetables are also shaped like spheres. You can shell a pod of green peas. Shred a head of cabbage. Top a salad with cherry tomatoes.

Peas may be the oldest vegetable on Earth. They are so old, even scientists do not know which country grew them first.

Spheres 13

SWEET SPHERES

Some spheres taste sweet. Chocolate candy comes wrapped in foil, covered in nuts, or inside a shiny coat of color. When you bite into it, what do you find inside? The chocolate might be hiding a caramel, marshmallow, or cherry center.

Lick a lemon lollipop and watch your tongue turn yellow. Set your mouth on fire with fireballs. Can giant jawbreakers really break your jaws? Chew bubble gum balls. Then, blow a big round bubble.

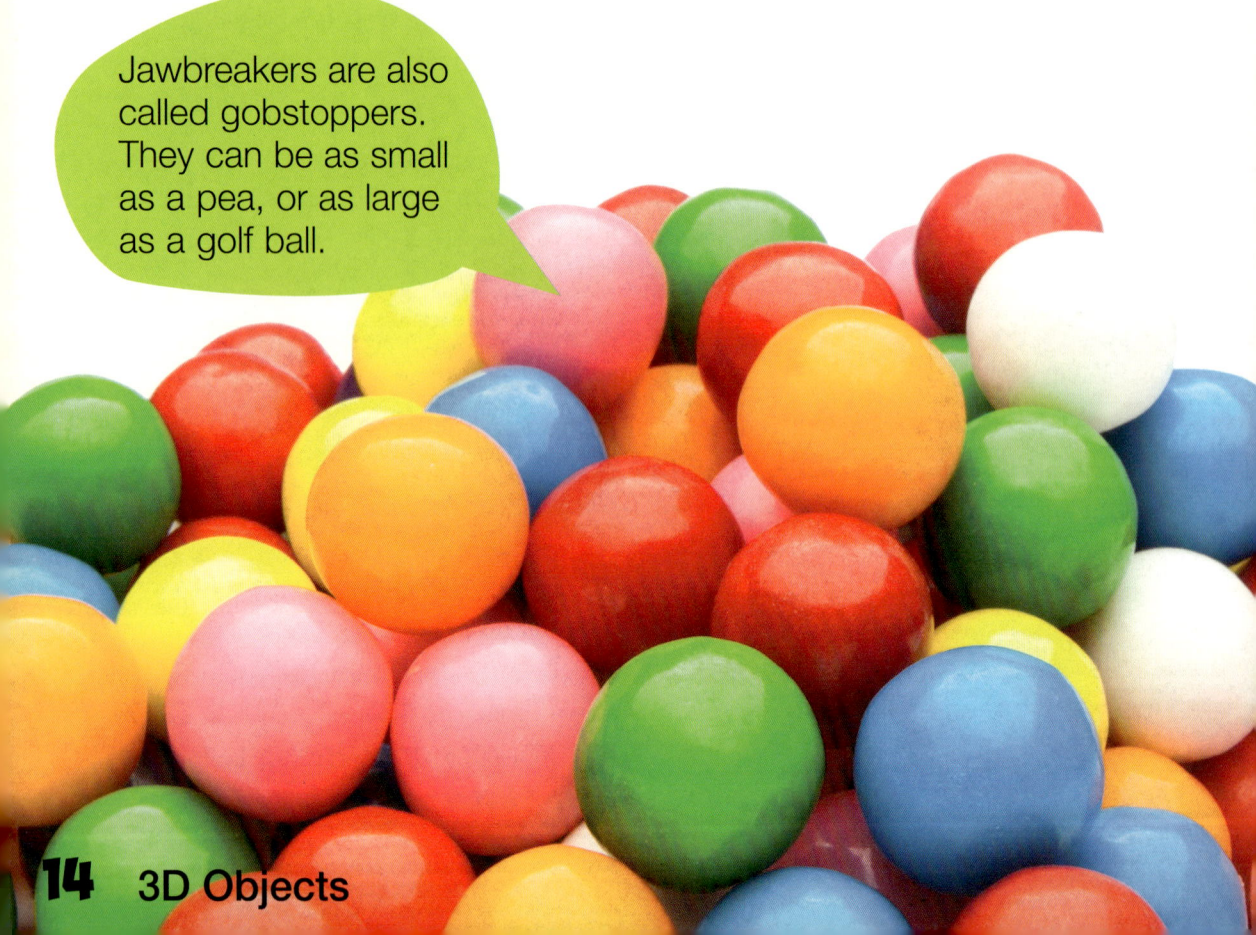

Jawbreakers are also called gobstoppers. They can be as small as a pea, or as large as a golf ball.

LARGEST BUBBLE GUM BUBBLE BLOWN

According to Guinness World Records, a man blew the world's biggest bubble gum bubble without using his hands in 2004. The bubble measured 20 inches (50.8 centimeters) in **diameter**. That is the size of a beach ball.

More gum is chewed in Iran than any other country in the world.

Spheres

BUILDING SPHERES

Some buildings are shaped like spheres. Perhaps the most famous is Spaceship Earth at Walt Disney World's Epcot Center. Riders spiral up 18 stories on a time-machine adventure. This 16-million-pound (7-million-kilogram) sphere looks like a giant silver golf ball.

Another sphere has found a second life in Canada. The Montreal Biosphere dome starred in that city's 1967 World Fair. Today, this steel sphere houses a museum.

Spaceship Earth is shaped like a sphere, but it is actually made out of 11,520 small triangles.

3D Objects

SPHERES IN SPACE

Did you know our planet Earth is a huge sphere? Our planet has been described as a "blue marble." It appears blue because most of Earth is covered with water. Look at a globe. You can see that 70 percent of Earth's surface is covered in water.

The eight planets in our solar system are all shaped like spheres. **Gravity** causes planets to form this shape. Every point on the planet's surface is pulled evenly toward the center. The result is a sphere shape.

Search for sphere shapes wherever you go. You can find these 3D shapes everywhere, here on Earth and out of this world.

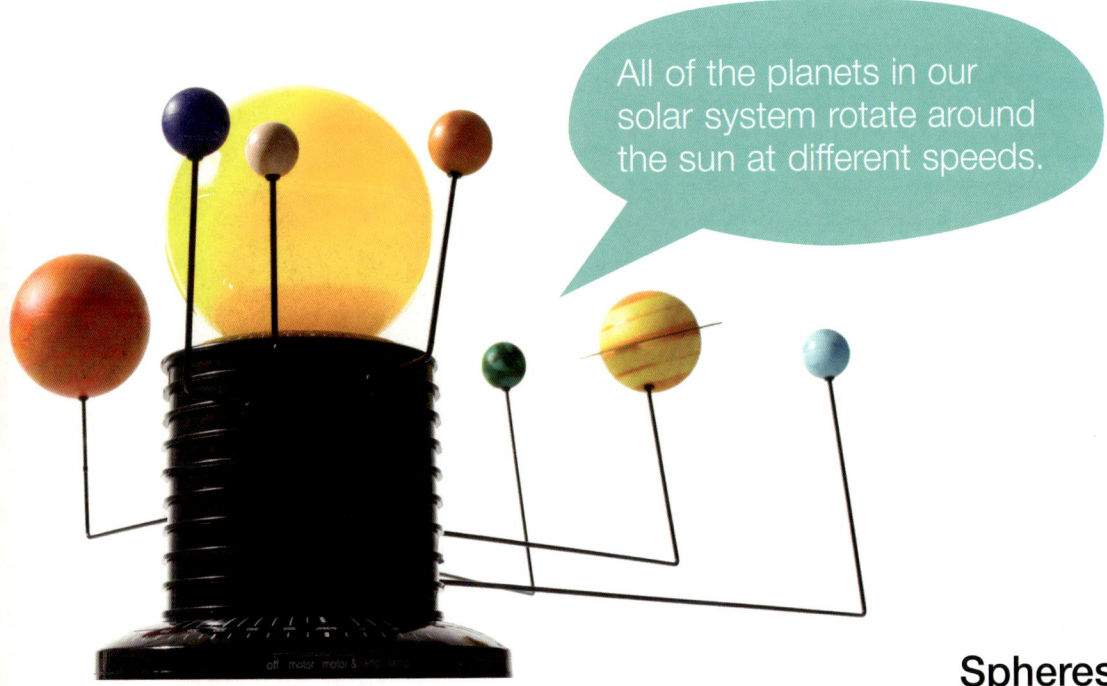

All of the planets in our solar system rotate around the sun at different speeds.

Spheres 17

SPHERES FOR ALL SEASONS

Spheres appear in every season. In the winter, we shake snow globes and watch flakes swirl around the scenes inside. Outside, we shape snow into spheres. Stack up three to make a snowman.

In the spring, flowers such as **allium** and fluffy, white dandelions grow in the shape of a sphere. Some people trim their shrubs into sphere shapes.

Snow is easy to shape into a sphere. If you roll a snowball on the ground, it gets bigger and bigger.

18 3D Objects

In the summer, we go to the beach. We play catch with a giant beach ball. On a pebbly beach, look for a stone that is perfectly round. Can you find one?

In the fall, we trick-or-treat on Halloween. We hope to bring home mounds of round candy. Later, we share popcorn balls. What a yummy snack.

Beach balls are spheres filled with air. They are light, and will not sink in the water.

Spheres

SPHERES QUIZ

1. How many edges and corners does a sphere have?

2. What is the oldest type of vegetable on Earth?

3. What are two flowers that grow into a sphere shape in spring?

4. Why does Earth appear blue from space?

3D Objects

5 What shapes make up Spaceship Earth?

6 What are some materials used to make marbles?

7 What was the game of jacks originally called?

8 What causes planets to be sphere-shaped?

Answers:
1. None 2. Peas 3. Allium and dandelions
4. Most of it is covered in water 5. Triangles
6. Glass, clay, stone, and marble 7. Knucklebones 8. Gravity

Spheres **21**

ACTIVITY: BUBBLE FUN

Mix up this homemade bubble solution. Then, wave the wand and watch your bubbles take flight.

Materials

- 2-1/2 quarts water
- 1/2 cup light corn syrup
- 1 cup clear liquid dish detergent
- food coloring
- spoon
- pail
- clothes hanger
- pliers
- cotton twine or yarn
- pie tin

Directions

1. Stir together the water and corn syrup in a pail. Add the liquid dish detergent and gently stir. You can make colored bubbles by adding a few drops of food coloring.

2. Make a wand. Have an adult help you unravel the hanger using pliers. Bend one end of the wire into a loop shape. Cover this shape with the twine or yarn. Bend the other end into a handle.

3. Pour the soap bubble solution into the pie tin.

4. Dip the loop end of the wand into the solution. Wave the wand and watch your soap bubbles soar.

22 3D Objects

KEY WORDS

3D: a shape with length, width, and height

allium: a large, round flower in the onion family

diameter: a straight line running from one side of a circle through the center to the other side

dimensions: the length, width, or height of an object

edges: the lines where a surface begins or ends

gravity: the force that pulls objects toward the center of Earth and other stars and planets

plane: a flat surface

produce: fruits and vegetables

spheres: 3D shapes that are rounded like a globe

surface: the flat or curved border of a 3D shape

INDEX

balls 4, 5, 6, 8, 10, 11, 14, 15, 16, 19
bubble gum 14, 15
bubbles 10, 14, 15, 22
buildings 16

candy 14, 19
center 8, 14, 16, 17
circles 6
corners 8, 9, 20

dimensions 6
Earth 13, 16, 17, 20, 21
edges 8, 9, 20

juggler 4

marbles 10, 11, 17, 21

points 8, 17

surface 8, 17

Spheres **23**

Log on to www.av2books.com

AV² by Weigl brings you media enhanced books that support active learning. Go to www.av2books.com, and enter the special code found on page 2 of this book. You will gain access to enriched and enhanced content that supplements and complements this book. Content includes video, audio, weblinks, quizzes, a slide show, and activities.

AV² Online Navigation

Book Pages
AV² pages directly correspond to pages in the book.

Audio
Listen to section the book read a

Video
Watch informat video clips.

Embedded Weblin
Gain additional informatio for research.

Try This!
Complete activities and hands-on experiments.

Key Words
Study vocabulary, and complete a matching word activity.

Quizzes
Test your knowledge.

Slide Show
View images and captions, and prepare a presentation.

AV² was built to bridge the gap between print and digital. We encourage you to tell us what you like and what you want to see in the future.

Sign up to be an AV² Ambassador at www.av2books.com/ambassador.

Due to the dynamic nature of the Internet, some of the URLs and activities provided as part of AV² by Weigl may have changed or ceased to exist. AV² by Weigl accepts no responsibility for any such changes. All media enhanced books are regularly monitored to update addresses and sites in a timely manner. Contact AV² by Weigl at 1-866-649-3445 or av2books@weigl.com with any questions, comments, or feedback.